LEARNING WITH
DADDY

COUNTING BY 10'S

10 20
30 40

BY
T. LEE PRESLEY II

The Learning with Daddy Book collection is dedicated to all the Dads all over the world. And of course the Learning with Daddy collection is dedicated to all the children all over the globe. And this book collection is especially dedicated to all the children growing up without a Dad. I especially wanted to assure them that there is a father figure out here for all them. I mean, aren't they just a joy to the world and so eager to grasp and learn everything we have to offer them. So, as a son, father, godfather, and grandfather I give this special collection in hopes of sharing the experience I have been fortunate to share with my grandfathers', my father, my kids, grandchildren, nieces, nephews, godchildren, foster children, neighborhood children, etc, etc, etc, etc, and all the other kids out there.

Let's all do our part. Love the Kids.

10

20

30

40

50

70

100

10

COUNTING BY 10'S

20

30

40

50

70

100

I ENJOYED

LEARNING WITH
DADDY

COUNTING BY 10'S

MY NAME

....

Printed in Great Britain
by Amazon